The Key Facts™

on

I0469095

The United

Arab Emirates

Essential Information on the United

Arab Emirates

By Patrick W. Nee

The Internationalist®

www.internationalist.com

The Internationalist®

International Business, Investment, and Travel

Published by:

The Internationalist Publishing Company

96 Walter Street/ Suite 200

Boston, MA 02131, USA

Tel: 617-354-7722

www.internationalist.com

PN@internationalist.com

Table Of Contents

Chapter 1: Background

The Trucial States of the Persian Gulf coast granted the UK control of their defense and foreign affairs in 19th century treaties. In 1971, six of these states - Abu Dhabi, 'Ajman, Al Fujayrah, Ash Shariqah, Dubayy, and Umm al Qaywayn - merged to form the United Arab Emirates (UAE). They were joined in 1972 by Ra's al Khaymah. The UAE's per capita GDP is on par with those of leading West European nations. Its high oil revenues and its moderate foreign policy stance have allowed the UAE to play a vital role in the affairs of the region. For more than three decades, oil and global finance drove the UAE's economy. However, in 2008-09, the confluence of falling oil prices, collapsing real estate prices, and the international banking crisis hit the UAE especially hard. The UAE has essentially avoided the "Arab Spring" unrest seen elsewhere in the Middle East, though in March 2011, political activists and intellectuals signed a petition calling for greater public participation in governance that was widely circulated on the Internet. In an effort to stem potential further unrest, the government announced a multi-year, $1.6-billion infrastructure investment plan for the poorer northern Emirates.

Chapter 2: Geography

Location:

Middle East, bordering the Gulf of Oman and the Persian Gulf, between Oman and Saudi Arabia

Geographic coordinates:

24 00 N, 54 00 E

Map references:

Middle East

Area:

total: 83,600 sq km

country comparison to the world: 115

land: 83,600 sq km

water: 0 sq km

Area - comparative:

slightly smaller than Maine

Land boundaries:

total: 867 km

border countries: Oman 410 km, Saudi Arabia 457 km

Coastline:

1,318 km

Maritime claims:

territorial sea: 12 nm

contiguous zone: 24 nm

exclusive economic zone: 200 nm

> continental shelf: 200 nm or to the edge of the continental margin

Climate:

> desert; cooler in eastern mountains

Terrain:

> flat, barren coastal plain merging into rolling sand dunes of vast desert wasteland; mountains in east

Elevation extremes:

> lowest point: Persian Gulf 0 m
>
> highest point: Jabal Yibir 1,527 m

Natural resources:

> petroleum, natural gas

Land use:

> arable land: 0.77%
>
> permanent crops: 2.27%
>
> other: 96.96% (2005)

Irrigated land:

> 2,300 sq km (2003)

Total renewable water resources:

> 0.2 cu km (1997)

Freshwater withdrawal (domestic/industrial/agricultural):

> total: 2.3 cu km/yr (23%/9%/68%)
>
> per capita: 511 cu m/yr (2000)

Natural hazards:

> frequent sand and dust storms

Environment - current issues:

lack of natural freshwater resources compensated by desalination plants; desertification; beach pollution from oil spills

Environment - international agreements:

party to: Biodiversity, Climate Change, Climate Change-Kyoto Protocol, Desertification, Endangered Species, Hazardous Wastes, Marine Dumping, Ozone Layer Protection

signed, but not ratified: Law of the Sea

Geography - note:

strategic location along southern approaches to Strait of Hormuz, a vital transit point for world crude oil

Chapter 3: People and Society

Nationality:

> <u>noun</u>: Emirati(s)

> <u>adjective</u>: Emirati

Ethnic groups:

> Emirati 19%, other Arab and Iranian 23%, South Asian 50%, other expatriates (includes Westerners and East Asians) 8% (1982)

> <u>note</u>: less than 20% are UAE citizens (1982)

Languages:

> Arabic (official), Persian, English, Hindi, Urdu

Religions:

> Muslim (Islam - official) 96% (Shia 16%), other (includes Christian, Hindu) 4%

Population:

> 5,314,317 (July 2012 est.)

> <u>country comparison to the world</u>: 115

> <u>note</u>: estimate is based on the results of the 2005 census that included a significantly higher estimate of net immigration of non-citizens than previous estimates

Age structure:

> <u>0-14 years</u>: 20.5% (male 557,603/female 532,303)

> <u>15-24 years</u>: 14% (male 440,556/female 301,147)

> <u>25-54 years</u>: 61.6% (male 2,497,606/female 774,318)

> <u>55-64 years</u>: 3% (male 122,356/female 38,402)

65 years and over: 0.9% (male 31,942/female 18,084) (2012 est.)

Median age:

total: 30.2 years

male: 32.1 years

female: 25 years (2012 est.)

Population growth rate:

3.055% (2012 est.)

country comparison to the world: 9

Birth rate:

15.76 births/1,000 population (2012 est.)

country comparison to the world: 129

Death rate:

2.04 deaths/1,000 population (July 2012 est.)

country comparison to the world: 223

Net migration rate:

16.82 migrant(s)/1,000 population (2012 est.)

country comparison to the world: 5

Urbanization:

urban population: 84% of total population (2010)

rate of urbanization: 2.3% annual rate of change (2010-15 est.)

Major cities - population:

ABU DHABI (capital) 666,000 (2009)

Sex ratio:

at birth: 1.05 male(s)/female

under 15 years: 1.05 male(s)/female

15-64 years: 2.75 male(s)/female

65 years and over: 1.77 male(s)/female

total population: 2.19 male(s)/female (2011 est.)

Maternal mortality rate:

12 deaths/100,000 live births (2010)

country comparison to the world: 148

Infant mortality rate:

total: 11.59 deaths/1,000 live births

country comparison to the world: 135

male: 13.54 deaths/1,000 live births

female: 9.55 deaths/1,000 live births (2012 est.)

Life expectancy at birth:

total population: 76.71 years

country comparison to the world: 72

male: 74.12 years

female: 79.42 years (2012 est.)

Total fertility rate:

2.38 children born/woman (2012 est.)

country comparison to the world: 94

Health expenditures:

2.8% of GDP (2009)

country comparison to the world: 181

Physicians density:

1.93 physicians/1,000 population (2007)

Hospital bed density:

1.9 beds/1,000 population (2008)

Sanitation facility access:

improved:

urban: 98% of population

rural: 95% of population

total: 97% of population

unimproved:

urban: 2% of population

rural: 5% of population

total: 3% of population

HIV/AIDS - adult prevalence rate:

0.2% (2001 est.)

country comparison to the world: 103

HIV/AIDS - people living with HIV/AIDS:

NA

HIV/AIDS - deaths:

NA

Obesity - adult prevalence rate:

33.7% (2000)

country comparison to the world: 7

Education expenditures:

1.2% of GDP (2009)

country comparison to the world: 161

Literacy:

definition: age 15 and over can read and write

total population: 77.9%

male: 76.1%

female: 81.7% (2003 est.)

School life expectancy (primary to tertiary education):

total: 13 years

male: 13 years

female: 14 years (2009)

Unemployment, youth ages 15-24:

total: 12.1%

country comparison to the world: 90

male: 7.9%

female: 21.8% (2008)

Chapter 4: Government and Key Leaders

Country name:

> conventional long form: United Arab Emirates
>
> conventional short form: none
>
> local long form: Al Imarat al Arabiyah al Muttahidah
>
> local short form: none
>
> former: Trucial Oman, Trucial States
>
> abbreviation: UAE

Government type:

> federation with specified powers delegated to the UAE federal government and other powers reserved to member emirates

Capital:

> name: Abu Dhabi
>
> geographic coordinates: 24 28 N, 54 22 E
>
> time difference: UTC+4 (9 hours ahead of Washington, DC during Standard Time)

Administrative divisions:

> 7 emirates (imarat, singular - imarah); Abu Zaby (Abu Dhabi), 'Ajman, Al Fujayrah, Ash Shariqah (Sharjah), Dubayy (Dubai), Ra's al Khaymah, Umm al Qaywayn (Quwain)

Independence:

> 2 December 1971 (from the UK)

National holiday:

Independence Day, 2 December (1971)

Constitution:

2 December 1971; made permanent in 1996

Legal system:

mixed legal system of Islamic law and civil law

International law organization participation:

has not submitted an ICJ jurisdiction declaration; non-party state to the ICCt

Suffrage:

limited; note - rulers of the seven Emirates each select a proportion of voters for the Federal National Council (FNC) that together account for about 12 percent of the native Emirati population

Executive branch:

<u>chief of state</u>: President KHALIFA bin Zayid Al-Nuhayyan (since 3 November 2004), ruler of Abu Zaby (Abu Dhabi) (since 4 November 2004); Vice President and Prime Minister MUHAMMAD BIN RASHID Al-Maktum (since 5 January 2006)

<u>head of government</u>: Prime Minister and Vice President MUHAMMAD BIN RASHID Al-Maktum (since 5 January 2006); Deputy Prime Ministers SAIF bin Zayid Al-Nuhayyan (since 11 May 2009) and MANSUR bin Zayid Al-Nuhayyan (since 11 May 2009)

<u>cabinet</u>: Council of Ministers appointed by the president

note: there is also a Federal Supreme Council (FSC) composed of the seven emirate rulers; the FSC is the highest constitutional authority in the UAE; establishes general policies and sanctions federal legislation; meets four times a year; Abu Zaby (Abu Dhabi) and Dubayy (Dubai) rulers have effective veto power

elections: president and vice president elected by the FSC for five-year terms (no term limits) from among the seven FSC members; election last held 3 November 2004 upon the death of the UAE's Founding Father and first President ZAYID bin Sultan Al Nuhayyan (next election NA); prime minister and deputy prime minister appointed by the president

election results: KHALIFA bin Zayid Al-Nuhayyan elected president by a unanimous vote of the FSC; MUHAMMAD bin Rashid Al-Maktum unanimously affirmed vice president after the 2006 death of his brother Sheikh MAKTUM bin Rashid Al-Maktum

Legislative branch:

unicameral Federal National Council (FNC) or Majlis al-Ittihad al-Watani (40 seats; 20 members appointed by the rulers of the constituent states, 20 members elected to serve four-year terms);

elections: last held on 24 September 2011 (next to be held in 2015); note - the electoral college was expanded from 6,689 voters in the December 2006 election to 129,274 in the September 2011 election; elections for candidates rather than party lists; 469 candidates including 85 women ran for 20 contested FNC seats

election results: elected seats by emirate - Abu Dhabi 4, Dubai 4, Sharjah 3, Ras al-Khaimah 3, Ajman 2, Fujairah 2, Umm al-Quwain 2; note - number of appointed seats for each emirate are same as elected seats

Judicial branch:

Union Supreme Court (judges are appointed by the president)

Political parties and leaders:

none; political parties are not allowed

Political pressure groups and leaders:

NA

International organization participation:

ABEDA, AfDB (nonregional member), AFESD, AMF, BIS, CAEU, CICA, FAO, G-77, GCC, IAEA, IBRD, ICAO, ICC (national committees), ICRM, IDA, IDB, IFAD, IFC, IFRCS, IHO, ILO, IMF, IMO, IMSO, Interpol, IOC, IPU, ISO, ITSO, ITU, LAS, MIGA, NAM, OAPEC, OIC, OIF (observer), OPCW, OPEC, PCA, UN, UNCTAD, UNESCO, UNIDO, UPU, WCO, WHO, WIPO, WMO, WTO

Diplomatic representation in the US:

chief of mission: Ambassador Yusif bin Mani bin Said al-UTAYBA chancery: 3522 International Court NW, Suite 400, Washington, DC 20008

telephone: [1] (202) 243-2400

FAX: [1] (202) 243-2432

Diplomatic representation from the US:

chief of mission: Ambassador Michael H. CORBIN

embassy: Embassies District, Plot 38 Sector W59-02, Street No. 4, Abu Dhabi

mailing address: P. O. Box 4009, Abu Dhabi

telephone: [971] (2) 414-2200

FAX: [971] (2) 414-2603

consulate(s) general: Dubai

Key Leaders:

Pres.	**KHALIFA bin Zayid Al Nuhayyan**
Vice Pres.	**MUHAMMAD BIN RASHID Al Maktum**
Prime Min.	**MUHAMMAD BIN RASHID Al Maktum**
Dep. Prime Min.	**MANSUR bin Zayid Al Nuhayyan**
Dep. Prime Min.	**SAIF bin Zayid Al Nuhayyan**

Min. of Cabinet Affairs	Muhammad Abdallah al-GERGAWI
Min. of Culture, Youth, & Community Development	Abd al-Rahman Muhammad al-UWAIS
Min. of Defense	MUHAMMAD BIN RASHID Al Maktum
Min. of Economy	Sultan bin Saeed al-MANSURI
Min. of Education	Humaid Muhammad Ubayd al-QATAMI
Min. of Energy	Muhammad bin Dhain al-HAMILI
Min. of Environment & Water	Rashid Ahmed bin FAHD
Min. of Finance	HAMDAN bin Rashid Al Maktum
Min. of Foreign Affairs	ABDALLAH bin Zayid Al Nuhayyan

Min. of Foreign Trade	LUBNA al-Qasimi
Min. of Health	Hanif bin Hassan ALI
Min. of Higher Education & Scientific Research	NUHAYYAN bin Mubarak Al Nuhayyan
Min. of Interior	SAIF bin Zayid Al Nuhayyan
Min. of Justice	Hadef bin Juaan al-DHAHERI
Min. of Labor	Saqr Ghobash Saeed GHOBASH
Min. of Presidential Affairs	MANSUR bin Zayid Al Nuhayyan
Min. of Public Works	HAMDAN bin Mubarak Al Nuhayyan
Min. of Social Affairs	Mariam bint Muhammad Khalfan al-RUMI
Min. of State for Federal	Anwar Muhammad GARGASH

National Council Affairs	
Min. of State for Financial Affairs	Obaid Humaid al-TAYER
Min. of State for Foreign Affairs	Anwar Muhammad GARGASH
Min. of State Without Portfolio	Reem Ibrahim al-HASHEMI
Min. of State Without Portfolio	Maitha Salem al-SHAMSI
Governor, Central Bank	Sultan bin Nasir al-SUWAYDI
Ambassador to the US	Yusif bin Mani bin Said al-UTAYBA
Permanent Representative to the UN, New York	Ahmad Abd al-Rahman al-JARMAN

Flag description:

three equal horizontal bands of green (top), white, and black with a wider vertical red band on the hoist side; the flag incorporates all four Pan-Arab colors, which in this case represent fertility (green), neutrality (white), petroleum resources (black), and unity (red); red was the traditional color incorporated into all flags of the emirates before their unification

National symbol(s):

golden falcon

National anthem:

name: "Nashid al-watani al-imarati" (National Anthem of the UAE)

lyrics/music: AREF Al Sheikh Abdullah Al Hassan/Mohamad Abdel WAHAB

note: music adopted 1971, lyrics adopted 1996; Mohamad Abdel WAHAB also composed the music for the anthem of Tunisia

Chapter 5: Economy

Economy - overview:

The UAE has an open economy with a high per capita income and a sizable annual trade surplus. Successful efforts at economic diversification have reduced the portion of GDP based on oil and gas output to 25%. Since the discovery of oil in the UAE more than 30 years ago, the country has undergone a profound transformation from an impoverished region of small desert principalities to a modern state with a high standard of living. The government has increased spending on job creation and infrastructure expansion and is opening up utilities to greater private sector involvement. In April 2004, the UAE signed a Trade and Investment Framework Agreement with Washington and in November 2004 agreed to undertake negotiations toward a Free Trade Agreement with the US; however, those talks have not moved forward. The country's Free Trade Zones - offering 100% foreign ownership and zero taxes - are helping to attract foreign investors. The global financial crisis, tight international credit, and deflated asset prices constricted the economy in 2009. UAE authorities tried to blunt the crisis by increasing spending and boosting liquidity in the banking sector. The crisis hit Dubai hardest, as it was heavily exposed to depressed real estate prices. Dubai lacked sufficient cash to meet its debt obligations, prompting global concern about its solvency. The UAE Central Bank and Abu Dhabi-based banks bought the largest shares. In December 2009 Dubai received an additional $10 billion loan from the emirate of Abu Dhabi. Dependence on oil, a large expatriate workforce, and growing inflation pressures are significant long-term challenges. The UAE's strategic plan for the next few years focuses on diversification and creating more opportunities for nationals through improved education and increased private sector employment.

GDP (purchasing power parity):

$271.2 billion (2012 est.)

country comparison to the world: 50

$260.7 billion (2011 est.)

$247.8 billion (2010 est.)

note: data are in 2012 US dollars

GDP (official exchange rate):

$361.9 billion (2012 est.)

GDP - real growth rate:

4% (2012 est.)

country comparison to the world: 82

5.2% (2011 est.)

1.3% (2010 est.)

GDP - per capita (PPP):

$49,000 (2012 est.)

country comparison to the world: 13

$48,500 (2011 est.)

$47,500 (2010 est.)

note: data are in 2012 US dollars

GDP - composition by sector:

agriculture: 0.8%

industry: 56.1%

services: 43.1% (2012 est.)

Labor force:

4.337 million

country comparison to the world: 86

note: expatriates account for about 85% of the work force (2012 est.)

Labor force - by occupation:

agriculture: 7%

industry: 15%

services: 78% (2000 est.)

Unemployment rate:

2.4% (2001)

country comparison to the world: 20

Population below poverty line:

19.5% (2003)

Investment (gross fixed):

28.5% of GDP (2012 est.)

country comparison to the world: 25

Budget:

revenues: $130.3 billion

expenditures: $113.8 billion (2012 est.)

Taxes and other revenues:

36% of GDP (2012 est.)

country comparison to the world: 66

Budget surplus (+) or deficit (-):

4.5% of GDP (2012 est.)

country comparison to the world: 15

Public debt:

40.4% of GDP (2012 est.)

country comparison to the world: 86

45.9% of GDP (2011 est.)

Inflation rate (consumer prices):

1.1% (2012 est.)

country comparison to the world: 9

0.9% (2011 est.)

Stock of narrow money:

$80.53 billion (31 December 2012 est.)

country comparison to the world: 41

$71.9 billion (31 December 2011 est.)

Stock of broad money:

$234.7 billion (31 December 2012 est.)

country comparison to the world: 37

$224.8 billion (31 December 2011 est.)

Stock of domestic credit:

$313.7 billion (31 December 2012 est.)

$293.2 billion (31 December 2011 est.)

Market value of publicly traded shares:

$93.77 billion (31 December 2011)

country comparison to the world: 42

$104.7 billion (31 December 2010)

$109.6 billion (31 December 2009)

Agriculture - products:

dates, vegetables, watermelons; poultry, eggs, dairy products; fish

Industries:

petroleum and petrochemicals; fishing, aluminum, cement, fertilizers, commercial ship repair, construction materials, some boat building, handicrafts, textiles

Industrial production growth rate:

3.2% (2010 est.)

country comparison to the world: 95

Current account balance:

$26.76 billion (2012 est.)

country comparison to the world: 15

$30.65 billion (2011 est.)

Exports:

$300.6 billion (2012 est.)

country comparison to the world: 20

$281.6 billion (2011 est.)

Exports - commodities:

crude oil 45%, natural gas, reexports, dried fish, dates

Exports - partners:

Japan 16.2%, India 13.5%, Iran 10.9%, South Korea 5.6%, Thailand 5.5%, Singapore 4.4% (2011)

Imports:

$220.3 billion (2012 est.)

country comparison to the world: 24

$202.1 billion (2011 est.)

Imports - commodities:

machinery and transport equipment, chemicals, food

Imports - partners:

India 19.8%, China 13.7%, US 8.1%, Germany 4.6% (2011)

Reserves of foreign exchange and gold:

$43.77 billion (31 December 2012 est.)

country comparison to the world: 41

$37.27 billion (31 December 2011 est.)

Debt - external:

$158.9 billion (31 December 2012 est.)

country comparison to the world: 34

$156.3 billion (31 December 2011 est.)

Stock of direct foreign investment - at home:

$91.56 billion (31 December 2012 est.)

country comparison to the world: 42

$83.36 billion (31 December 2011 est.)

Stock of direct foreign investment - abroad:

$58.1 billion (31 December 2012 est.)

country comparison to the world: 33

$55.6 billion (31 December 2011 est.)

Exchange rates:

Emirati dirhams (AED) per US dollar -

3.673 (2012 est.)

3.673 (2011 est.)

3.6725 (2010 est.)

3.673 (2009)

3.6725 (2008)

Fiscal year:

calendar year

Chapter 6: Energy

Electricity - production:

> 83.31 billion kWh (2010 est.)

> country comparison to the world: 38

Electricity - consumption:

> 74.12 billion kWh (2009 est.)

> country comparison to the world: 38

Electricity - exports:

> 0 kWh (2010 est.)

> country comparison to the world: 154

Electricity - imports:

> 0 kWh (2010 est.)

> country comparison to the world: 154

Electricity - installed generating capacity:

> 23.25 million kW (2009 est.)

> country comparison to the world: 33

Electricity - from fossil fuels:

> 100% of total installed capacity (2009 est.)

> country comparison to the world: 47

Electricity - from nuclear fuels:

> 0% of total installed capacity (2009 est.)

> country comparison to the world: 35

Electricity - from hydroelectric plants:

> 0% of total installed capacity (2009 est.)

> country comparison to the world: 154

Electricity - from other renewable sources:

      0% of total installed capacity (2009 est.)

      country comparison to the world: 99

Crude oil - production:

      3.087 million bbl/day (2011 est.)

      country comparison to the world: 9

Crude oil - exports:

      2.036 million bbl/day (2009 est.)

      country comparison to the world: 7

Crude oil - imports:

      0 bbl/day (2009 est.)

      country comparison to the world: 148

Crude oil - proved reserves:

      97.8 billion bbl (1 January 2012 est.)

      country comparison to the world: 8

Refined petroleum products - production:

      346,900 bbl/day (2008 est.)

      country comparison to the world: 39

Refined petroleum products - consumption:

      572,100 bbl/day (2011 est.)

      country comparison to the world: 33

Refined petroleum products - exports:

      452,400 bbl/day (2008 est.)

      country comparison to the world: 17

Refined petroleum products - imports:

      377,300 bbl/day (2008 est.)

country comparison to the world: 17

Natural gas - production:

51.28 billion cu m (2010 est.)

country comparison to the world: 19

Natural gas - consumption:

60.54 billion cu m (2010 est.)

country comparison to the world: 14

Natural gas - exports:

7.65 billion cu m (2010 est.)

country comparison to the world: 27

Natural gas - imports:

16.91 billion cu m (2010 est.)

country comparison to the world: 18

Natural gas - proved reserves:

6.089 trillion cu m (1 January 2012 est.)

country comparison to the world: 8

Carbon dioxide emissions from consumption of energy:

199.4 million Mt (2010 est.)

country comparison to the world: 27

Chapter 7: Communications

Telephones - main lines in use:

    1.825 million (2011)

    <u>country comparison to the world</u>: 61

Telephones - mobile cellular:

    11.727 million (2011)

    <u>country comparison to the world</u>: 66

Telephone system:

    <u>general assessment</u>: modern fiber-optic integrated services; digital network with rapidly growing use of mobile-cellular telephones; key centers are Abu Dhabi and Dubai

    <u>domestic</u>: microwave radio relay, fiber optic and coaxial cable

    <u>international</u>: country code - 971; linked to the international submarine cable FLAG (Fiber-Optic Link Around the Globe); landing point for both the SEA-ME-WE-3 and SEA-ME-WE-4 submarine cable networks; satellite earth stations - 3 Intelsat (1 Atlantic Ocean and 2 Indian Ocean) and 1 Arabsat; tropospheric scatter to Bahrain; microwave radio relay to Saudi Arabia

Broadcast media:

    except for the many organizations now operating in Dubai's Media Free Zone, most TV and radio stations remain government-owned; widespread use of satellite dishes provides access to pan-Arab and other international broadcasts (2007)

Internet country code:

.ae

Internet hosts:

337,804 (2012)

country comparison to the world: 61

Internet users:

3.449 million (2009)

country comparison to the world: 61

Chapter 8: Transportation

Airports:

>42 (2012)

>country comparison to the world: 102

Airports - with paved runways:

>total: 25

>over 3,047 m: 12

>2,438 to 3,047 m: 3

>1,524 to 2,437 m: 4

>914 to 1,523 m: 4

>under 914 m: 2 (2012)

Airports - with unpaved runways:

>total: 17

>over 3,047 m: 1

>2,438 to 3,047 m: 1

>1,524 to 2,437 m: 4

>914 to 1,523 m: 6

>under 914 m: 5 (2012)

Heliports:

>5 (2012)

Pipelines:

>condensate 458 km; refined products 212 km; gas 2,352 km; liquid petroleum gas 220 km; oil 1,437 km (2010)

Roadways:

>total: 4,080 km

country comparison to the world: 157

paved: 4,080 km (includes 253 km of expressways) (2008)

Merchant marine:

total: 61

country comparison to the world: 65

by type: bulk carrier 3, cargo 13, chemical tanker 8, container 7, liquefied gas 1, passenger/cargo 1, petroleum tanker 24, roll on/roll off 4

foreign-owned: 13 (Greece 3, Kuwait 10)

registered in other countries: 253 (Bahamas 23, Barbados 1, Belize 3, Cambodia 2, Comoros 8, Cyprus 3, Georgia 2, Gibraltar 5, Honduras 1, Hong Kong 1, India 4, Iran 2, Jordan 2, Liberia 37, Malta 1, Marshall Islands 12, Mexico 1, Netherlands 4, North Korea 2, Panama 83, Papua New Guinea 6, Philippines 1, Saint Kitts and Nevis 8, Saint Vincent and the Grenadines 3, Saudi Arabia 6, Sierra Leone 1, Singapore 10, Tanzania 3, Togo 1, UK 8, Vanuatu 1, unknown 8) (2010)

Ports and terminals:

Al Fujayrah, Mina' Jabal 'Ali (Dubai), Khor Fakkan (Khawr Fakkan), Mubarraz Island, Mina' Rashid (Dubai), Mina' Saqr (Ra's al Khaymah)

Chapter 9: Military

Military branches:

>United Arab Emirates Armed Forces: Critical Infrastructure Coastal Patrol Agency (CNIA), Land Forces, Navy, Air Force and Air Defense, Border and Coast Guard Directorate (BCGD) (2012)

Military service age and obligation:

>18 years of age for voluntary military service; 18 years of age for officers and women; no conscription; 16-22 years of age for candidates for the UAE Naval College (2009)

Manpower available for military service:

>males age 16-49: 2,676,928 (includes non-nationals)
>
>females age 16-49: 981,649 (2010 est.)

Manpower fit for military service:

>males age 16-49: 2,229,366
>
>females age 16-49: 842,759 (2010 est.)

Manpower reaching militarily significant age annually:

>male: 27,439
>
>female: 24,419 (2010 est.)

Military expenditures:

>3.1% of GDP (2005 est.)
>
>country comparison to the world: 38

Chapter 10: Transnational Issues

Disputes - international:

boundary agreement was signed and ratified with Oman in 2003 for entire border, including Oman's Musandam Peninsula and Al Madhah enclaves, but contents of the agreement and detailed maps showing the alignment have not been published; Iran and UAE dispute Tunb Islands and Abu Musa Island, which Iran occupies

Illicit drugs:

the UAE is a drug transshipment point for traffickers given its proximity to Southwest Asian drug-producing countries; the UAE's position as a major financial center makes it vulnerable to money laundering; anti-money-laundering controls improving, but informal banking remains unregulated

Other Key Facts™ Titles

All Key Facts™ Titles are

Available at www.Amazon.com

THE INTERNATIONALIST®

2013

www.internationalist.com